Travel Guide to Osaka 2024"

"Practical information about Osaka and Itinerary for all kinds of travellers "

Judith G. Harrison

Judith G Harrison

Judith G Harrison

TABLE OF CONTENTS

Judith G Harrison

Judith G Harrison

Judith G Harrison

WELCOME TO OSAKA

My journey to Osaka, the vibrant heart of Japan, was an experience that will live on in my memories as a traveller forever. Whether it was in the crowded alleys of Dotonbori or the tranquil gardens of Osaka Castle, every moment was a great discovery just waiting to be made.

My taste receptors were mesmerised by the gastronomic delicacies of Osaka like never before. In addition to being delicious dishes, the sizzling takoyaki, crispy okonomiyaki, and

Judith G Harrison

melt-in-your-mouth Kobe beef were sensory symphonies. My culinary journey led me from modest street vendors to Michelin-starred eateries, demonstrating the city's ingrained culinary tradition and a gastronomic tapestry that would satisfy even the pickiest eater.

I had the impression that I was a character in a vibrant anime universe as I walked through the Dotonbori neighbourhood's neon-lit streets. Osaka's lively and creative attitude was seen in the classic Glico Running Man sign and the captivating mechanical crab. Every stroll was an exciting experience, with a new gastronomic treat or exciting street performance waiting around every corner.

Exploring the ancient *Osaka Castle* was one of the most romantic parts of my trip. The castle, which was surrounded by cherry blossoms that were in full bloom, served as a reminder of

Japan's lengthy past. I received panoramic views of the city after making the ascent to the summit, and I couldn't help but be in awe of Osaka's flawless fusion of the old and the contemporary.

My day travels to Kyoto, Nara, and Kobe gave my journey more dimension. I strolled through Kyoto's tranquil Arashiyama Bamboo Grove and gawked at Kinkaku-ji, also known as the Golden Pavilion, for its complex beauty. The towering Great Buddha of Todai-ji Temple left me in awe of ancient craftsmanship in Nara, where friendly deer grazed freely. I learned

Judith G Harrison

about the craft of sake-making on a trip to a sake brewery on Kobe's picturesque Mount Rokko.

Every day ended with a feeling of accomplishment and awe. My nights in Osaka were as exciting as my days thanks to the city's thriving nightlife. The nights were as varied as the city itself, whether I was taking in the lively Namba quarter or enjoying cocktails at a rooftop bar with expansive city views.

I felt at home among the Osaka residents because to their gracious hospitality. They were willing to engage in polite talks, impart knowledge, and suggest undiscovered gems. I was able to fully grasp Osaka's heart and spirit thanks to these interactions.

I thought back on the amazing experiences and memories that made up my Osaka vacation as I

Judith G Harrison

boarded my journey home. My traveller's heart was forever changed by the city's harmonious blend of heritage and modernity, its delicious cuisine, and its vibrant culture. Osaka was no longer just a place to go; it had evolved into a priceless memory that I would always cherish, a symbol of the wonder of travel and the allure of adventure.

INTRODUCTION

Why Visit Osaka

SHOPPING PARADISE: Shopping in Osaka is a shopping lover's dream, offering everything from upscale department stores to conventional markets. Everything is available, including luxury clothing, electronics, and mementos.

Judith G Harrison

FOOD: Osaka is known for its delicious food, and there are endless opportunities to try new and exciting dishes. From takoyaki (octopus balls) and okonomiyaki (savoury pancakes) to sushi and tempura, you're sure to find something to your taste.

HISTORY AND CULTURE:

History and culture Osaka has a lengthy history that dates back to the sixth century. There are many historical places to see, like the Dotombori neighbourhood and Osaka Castle.

Judith G Harrison

NIGHTLIFE: Everyone may find something to enjoy in Osaka's thriving nightlife. You're sure to enjoy a memorable night, whether you choose izakayas (Japanese pubs), clubs, or karaoke bars.

THEME PARKS: There are various theme parks in Osaka, including DisneySea and Universal Studios Japan. For people of all ages, these parks provide hours of entertainment.

THE GEISHA CULTURE: One of the few remaining geisha viewing locations in Japan is

Judith G Harrison

in Osaka. These traditional Japanese performers give viewers a look into Japanese culture.

HOT SPRINGS (ONSEN): Osaka is home to a large number of onsen. The natural hot springs here are a wonderful place to unwind and revitalise.

CHERRY BLOSSOMS: When the cherry blossoms are in bloom in the spring, Osaka is a stunning city. Because it's a popular time to travel, make sure you reserve your lodging in advance.

Judith G Harrison

SUMO FIGHTING: The Dotombori Grand Sumo Tournament is held in Osaka twice a year in the spring and the autumn. The chance to watch sumo wrestlers in action is fantastic.

PEOPLE: Osakans are known for their friendly and welcoming nature. They are always happy to help visitors and make them feel at home.

How to Use This Guide

Welcome to the "Travel Guide to Osaka ." This guide has been meticulously crafted to help you make the most of your visit to Osaka, Japan's bustling metropolis. To navigate your journey effectively, follow these guidelines on how to make the most of this comprehensive resource:

1. Start with the Introduction:

Judith G Harrison

- Begin by reading the introduction section to get a feel for what Osaka has to offer and why it's an exciting destination for your 2023/2024 trip.

2. Plan Your Trip:

- Chapter 1 provides essential information for planning your trip, including when to visit, visa requirements, budgeting tips, packing advice, and the importance of travel insurance.

3. Where To Stay

- Chapter 3 provides you with complete information about accommodations no matter your budget.

4. Explore Top Attractions:

- Chapter 4 is your guide to Osaka's must-visit attractions. Learn about iconic places like Osaka Castle, Dotonbori, and

Judith G Harrison

more, along with practical information on how to reach them.

5. Savour Osaka's Food Scene:

- Chapter 5 is dedicated to Osaka's renowned culinary culture. Discover must-try dishes, where to find the best street food, top restaurants, and dining experiences unique to Osaka.

6. Shop Around Osaka:

- Chapter 5 explores Osaka's shopping scene, from traditional markets to modern malls. Find the perfect souvenirs and gifts while learning about the best places to indulge in retail therapy.

7. Experience Nightlife and Entertainment:

- Chapter 6 is your guide to Osaka's vibrant nightlife, including bars, nightclubs, theatres, and a rundown of festivals and events you won't want to miss.

8. Outdoor and Recreational Activities:

- Chapter 7 highlights outdoor adventures, including parks, gardens, cycling tours, and other recreational activities that allow you to enjoy Osaka's natural beauty.

9. Day Trips from Osaka:

- Chapter 8 provides information on day trips to nearby cities like Kyoto, Nara, Kobe, Hiroshima, and Miyajima Island, expanding your exploration beyond Osaka.

10. Practical Information:

- In Chapter 9, find essential details on transportation within Osaka, visitor cards

Judith G Harrison

and passes, currency exchange, safety tips, internet connectivity, and local etiquette.

By following this guide step by step, you'll be well-prepared to embark on an exciting adventure in Osaka, making the most of your time in this captivating Japanese city. Whether you're a history buff, a foodie, a shopper, or an outdoor enthusiast, Osaka has something remarkable in store for you. Enjoy your journey.

Tips for Travelling in Osaka

Osaka, with its unique blend of tradition and modernity, offers travellers an unforgettable

Judith G Harrison

experience. To make your trip to this vibrant Japanese city smooth and enjoyable, consider these valuable tips:

1. Learn Basic Japanese Phrases:

- While many people in Osaka's tourist areas speak English, knowing a few basic Japanese phrases like greetings and thank you can go a long way in enhancing your interactions with locals.

2. Use an IC Card:

- Purchase an IC card (e.g., ICOCA, Suica, or Pasmo) for convenient access to public transportation, including trains and buses. These cards can also be used for small purchases at convenience stores and vending machines.

3. Respect Local Customs:

- Japanese culture places a strong emphasis on etiquette and respect. Bowing is a common form of greeting, and it's polite to remove your shoes before entering someone's home or certain traditional establishments.

4. Carry Cash:

- While credit cards are accepted at many places in Osaka, it's advisable to carry some Japanese yen in cash, especially for small purchases and in more traditional establishments that may not accept cards.

5. Use Google Maps and Translation Apps:

- Download map and translation apps on your phone before your trip. Google Maps is particularly useful for navigating public transportation, while translation apps can help bridge language barriers.

Judith G Harrison

6. Get a Japan Rail Pass:

- If you plan to explore multiple cities in Japan, consider getting a Japan Rail Pass before your trip. This pass allows unlimited travel on Japan Railways (JR) lines, making it cost-effective for long-distance journeys.

7. Follow Train Etiquette:

- When using public transportation, maintain silence, and avoid talking on the phone. Priority seating is reserved for elderly, disabled, and pregnant passengers, so be mindful of this.

8. Try Street Food:

- Osaka is famous for its street food. Don't hesitate to try local delicacies like takoyaki (octopus balls), okonomiyaki (savory pancakes), and kushikatsu (deep-fried skewers) from street vendors.

Judith G Harrison

9. Budget Wisely:

- Set a budget for your trip and stick to it. Osaka offers options for all budgets, so whether you're looking for affordable street food or a gourmet dining experience, plan your expenses accordingly.

10. Stay Connected:

- Purchase a SIM card or portable Wi-Fi device to stay connected to the internet while exploring Osaka. This will help you navigate, access information, and stay in touch with loved ones.

11. Be Punctual:

- Japanese transportation runs on a strict schedule, so be punctual when catching trains or buses. Arriving a few minutes

Judith G Harrison

early will ensure you don't miss your ride.

12. Embrace Osaka's Nightlife:

- Osaka comes alive at night. Explore the city's vibrant nightlife by visiting local bars, izakayas (Japanese pubs), and entertainment districts like Dotonbori.

CHAPTER 1: PLANNING YOUR TRIP

Best time to Visit Osaka

The best time to visit Osaka largely depends on your preferences for weather and seasonal attractions. Osaka experiences distinct seasons, each offering a unique charm:

Judith G Harrison

SPRING (MARCH TO MAY): Spring is arguably the best time to visit Osaka. The city bursts into a riot of cherry blossoms (sakura) during late March to early April, creating a picturesque landscape. Mild temperatures and clear skies make it ideal for outdoor activities, and this season also coincides with various festivals, adding to the vibrant atmosphere.

SUMMER (JUNE TO AUGUST): Summers in Osaka are hot and humid, with occasional rain showers. If you can tolerate the heat and humidity, you'll find plenty of summer festivals

Judith G Harrison

and events. However, be prepared for the possibility of typhoons and heavy rainfall.

AUTUMN (SEPTEMBER TO NOVEMBER): Autumn is another excellent time to visit Osaka. The weather is pleasant, and the city's parks and gardens showcase beautiful fall foliage. It's a great time for sightseeing, with fewer crowds compared to spring.

WINTER (DECEMBER TO FEBRUARY): Winters in Osaka are relatively mild, although it can get chilly. This is the season for illuminations and holiday festivities, including Christmas markets and New Year celebrations. While it's not the best time for outdoor activities, you can still enjoy the city's indoor attractions and delicious hot pot dishes.

Ultimately, the best time to visit Osaka depends on your personal preferences for weather and

Judith G Harrison

the types of activities and events you wish to experience during your trip. Whether you prefer cherry blossoms in spring or autumn foliage, Osaka has something to offer year-round.

Visa and Entry Requirements

Citizens of most countries need a visa to enter Japan, including Osaka. However, citizens of 65 countries are visa-exempt for tourism or business purposes for a stay of up to 90 days. These countries include:

Judith G Harrison

European Union countries: Austria, Belgium, Bulgaria, Croatia, Cyprus, Czech Republic, Denmark, Estonia, Finland, France, Germany, Greece, Hungary, Iceland, Ireland, Italy, Latvia, Liechtenstein, Lithuania, Luxembourg, Malta, Netherlands, Poland, Portugal, Romania, Slovakia, Slovenia, Spain, Sweden, and United Kingdom.

North America: Canada, Mexico, and United States.

South America: Argentina, Brazil, Chile, Colombia, Ecuador, Peru, and Uruguay.

Asia: Australia, Brunei, Hong Kong, Indonesia, Israel, Macau, Malaysia, Mongolia, New Zealand, Singapore, South Korea, Taiwan, and Thailand.

Africa: Morocco and Tunisia.

Judith G Harrison

Oceania: Fiji, Micronesia, Nauru, Palau, Papua New Guinea, Samoa, Solomon Islands, Tonga, and Vanuatu.

If you are a citizen of a visa-exempt country, you will still need to have a valid passport and an onward or return ticket when you enter Japan. You may also be asked to provide proof of financial support.

The entry documents required for a vacation tourist to enter Osaka are:

- A valid passport
- A recent passport photo
- Proof of onward or return travel
- Proof of financial support

You may also be asked to provide a letter of invitation from a Japanese citizen or resident (if applicable).

Judith G Harrison

You can find more information about visa requirements and entry documents on the website of the Japanese Ministry of Foreign Affairs.

Here are some additional things to keep in mind when entering Osaka:

- You must have a valid passport and an onward or return ticket.
- You may be asked to provide proof of financial support.
- You may be asked to answer questions about your purpose of visit.
- You may be asked to have your fingerprints and photograph taken.

If you have any questions about visa requirements or entry documents for Osaka, you

Judith G Harrison

can contact the nearest Japanese embassy or consulate.

Travel Budgeting

The cost of travelling to Osaka can vary depending on your budget, the time of year you travel, and your activities. However, here is a rough estimate of how much you can expect to spend on a trip to Osaka:

Accommodation: A hostel bed will cost around $20-30 per night, while a hotel room will cost around $50-100 per night.

Food: Eating at local restaurants will cost around $10-15 per meal, while eating at more expensive restaurants will cost around $20-30 per meal.

Transportation: The subway is the most efficient way to get around Osaka, and a single fare costs around $2.

Attractions: Admission to popular attractions, such as Osaka Castle and Dotonbori district, costs around $10-20.

Other expenses: This could include things like souvenirs, laundry, and tipping.

So, if you are on a tight budget, you could expect to spend around $100-150 per day on your trip to Osaka. If you are willing to spend more, you could easily spend $200-300 per day.

Here are some tips for saving money on your trip to Osaka:

- Stay in a hostel.
- Eat at local restaurants.

Judith G Harrison

- Use the subway instead of taxis.
- Visit attractions during off-peak hours.
- Buy a tourist pass, which can save you money on transportation and attractions.

Packing Tips

Here are some Osaka travel packing tips:

Comfortable shoes: You will be doing a lot of walking in Osaka, so comfortable shoes are essential.

Lightweight clothing: The weather in Osaka is warm and humid, so pack light, breathable clothing.

Rain gear: It rains occasionally in Osaka, so pack a rain jacket and umbrella.

Judith G Harrison

Sunglasses and hat: The sun can be strong in Osaka, so pack sunglasses and a hat to protect yourself from the sun.

Camera: Osaka is a beautiful city, so you'll want to bring a camera to capture your memories.

Money belt: A money belt is a safe way to carry your passport, money, and other valuables.

Universal adapter: Osaka uses a different type of electrical outlet than most countries, so you'll need a universal adapter to charge your devices.

Travel insurance: Travel insurance can help you cover unexpected expenses, such as medical bills or lost luggage.

Here are some additional tips:

- Pack layers so you can adjust to the weather.
- If you are visiting during the winter, pack warmer clothes.
- Be aware of the cultural norms in Japan and dress accordingly.

Judith G Harrison

Travel Insurance

While not legally required in Japan, experts strongly advise all visitors to invest in travel medical insurance before their journey. Without it, the financial burden of any necessary medical treatment abroad may rest solely on your shoulders.

The benefits of travel insurance include:

Medical Coverage: Ensuring medical expenses, such as doctor's visits, hospital stays, and surgeries, are covered during your stay in Japan.

Trip Cancellation or Interruption: Providing coverage for trip cancellations or interruptions due to reasons like illness, injury, or natural disasters.

Judith G Harrison

Baggage Loss or Damage: Reimbursing you for lost or damaged luggage.

Emergency Medical Evacuation: Covering the expenses for transportation back to your home country if specialised medical care is required in Japan.

Lost Passport or Visa: Reimbursing you for the cost of replacing lost or stolen travel documents.

When selecting a travel insurance plan, carefully review the policy details to ensure it covers your intended activities in Japan and offers adequate coverage limits for major medical emergencies.

Here are some reputable travel insurance providers:

Judith G Harrison

- World Nomads
- Travel Guard
- InsuranceBee
- SafetyWing
- AIG Travel

You can conveniently compare plans and request quotes online. Prioritising travel insurance will grant you peace of mind and financial security during your Japanese adventure.

Chapter 2: Top Attractions in Osaka

Osaka Castle

Osaka Castle, often referred to as "Osaka-jo" in Japanese, is a memorial honouring Japan's long and rich history. This beautiful fortification in Chuo-ku, Osaka, is a symbol of endurance and tenacity that has withstood centuries of change.

Toyotomi Hideyoshi, one of Japan's most powerful feudal lords, constructed Osaka Castle in the late 16th century, and it played a significant role in the history of that country. It was an important site for culture, a military stronghold, and a political hub.

Judith G Harrison

The building of the castle includes magnificent woodwork carvings, high stone walls, and a commanding presence that harkens back to the samurai era. Despite the fact that fires and conflicts significantly damaged the previous structure, the new reconstruction successfully preserves the castle's historic features.

Visitors may now study about feudal Japan in the magnificent Osaka Castle interior while also admiring the broad views from the observation deck. It is a must-see sight that brilliantly encapsulates Osaka's rich history and fortitude.

Judith G Harrison

practical information on how to get to Osaka Castle

By train: The nearest train station to Osaka Castle is Osakajo-koen Station, which is served by the JR Osaka Loop Line and the Osaka Metro Tanimachi Line. The station is about a 10-minute walk from the castle. The fare from Osaka Station is 240 JPY (about 2 USD) for adults and 120 JPY (about 1 USD) for children.

By bus: There are also several bus lines that stop near Osaka Castle. The fare is 230 JPY (about 2 USD) for adults and 110 JPY (about 1 USD) for children.

By bicycle: If you are staying in the city centre, you can also rent a bicycle and ride to Osaka Castle. The rental fee is around 500 JPY (about 5 USD) per day.

Judith G Harrison

Once you arrive at Osakajo-koen Station, follow the signs to Osaka Castle. The castle is open from 9:00 AM to 5:00 PM, and the admission fee is 600 JPY (about 5 USD) for adults and 300 JPY (about 3 USD) for children.

Here are some tips for visiting Osaka Castle:

- Buy your tickets online or at the station in advance to avoid the long lines at the ticket booth.
- Visit the castle early in the morning or late in the afternoon to avoid the crowds.
- Wear comfortable shoes as there is a lot of walking involved.
- Allow at least 2 hours to explore the castle and its grounds.

Judith G Harrison

Dotonbori Entertainment District: The Pulse of Osaka

In the heart of Osaka, the Dotonbori Entertainment District is a thriving centre of cuisine, culture, and exciting activities. This well-known neighbourhood along the Dotonbori Canal is a smaller version of Osaka's vibrant personality.

Food Wonderland A culinary haven, Dotonbori is home to a bewildering array of eateries, from street vendors selling delicious takoyaki (octopus balls) to elegant Michelin-starred institutions. You may enjoy regional favourites

Judith G Harrison

like okonomiyaki and kushikatsu while taking in the stunning neon nighttime lighting.

theatrical encounters Dotonbori is home to renowned theatres like the Namba Grand Kagetsu, where you can see comedic performances like the well-known manzai stand-up comedy.

In "Neon Dreams," the neon billboards and signs in the neighbourhood create a mesmerising nocturnal backdrop. Take pictures of the famous Glico Running Man sign and the mechanical Kani Doraku Crab show for amazing photo opportunities.

When exploring the bustling alleys lined with stores, arcades, and karaoke bars in Dotonbori, there is never a boring moment.

Dotonbori is more than simply a fun area to hang out; it's also a sensory overload, a culinary adventure, and a symbol of Osaka's unrestrained life. Anyone taking in the city's lively culture, day or night, must make the stop.

Shitenno-ji Temple

Osaka's Shitenno-ji Temple, which dates back to the 6th century, is one of Japan's oldest and most revered Buddhist temples. It possesses enormous cultural and spiritual value and was established by Prince Shotoku, a significant figure in Japanese Buddhism.

In the midst of the busy metropolis, the temple's architectural splendour, which is characterised by conventional wooden constructions and a five-story pagoda, emanates a calm aura. Shitenno-ji, which is devoted to the Four Heavenly Kings, has a main hall, a lecture hall, and lovely gardens that invite guests to explore.

Shitenno-ji Temple welcomes both pilgrims and tourists to enjoy its historical significance, tranquillity, and the spiritual energy that

Judith G Harrison

permeates its hallowed boundaries as a site of worship and thought. It is a symbol of Japan's continuing Buddhist legacy and a must-see location for anybody interested in learning more about the diverse cultural heritage of the nation. *Here is the practical information on how to get to Shitenno-ji Temple.*

By train: The temple is a short walk from Shitennoji-mae Yuhigaoka Station on the Osaka Metro Tanimachi Line. The fare is 250 yen (about $2.25) for a single journey. Exit the station at exit 4 and walk straight ahead for about 5 minutes.

By subway: The temple is also a 10-minute walk north of Tennoji Station on the JR Osaka Loop Line. The fare is 220 yen (about $2) for a single journey. From Tennoji Station, take the north exit and walk straight ahead for about 10 minutes.

Judith G Harrison

The entrance fee to the temple is 300 yen (about $2.75) for adults, 200 yen (about $1.80) for senior high and university students, and free for children of junior high age or younger.

The temple is open from 8:30am to 4:30pm, from April to September, and from 9:00am to 4:00pm, from October to March.

Universal Studios Japan

The exciting theme park Universal Studios Japan, which is based in Osaka, offers the allure of Hollywood to Japan. USJ provides visitors of all ages with an amazing experience with its immersive attractions, breathtaking shows, and well-known movie characters.

Judith G Harrison

At The Wizarding World of Harry Potter, you may explore Hogwarts Castle, drink butterbeer, and even ride the famed Hogwarts Express as you enter the enchanted world of Harry Potter. Heart-pounding thrills like the Hollywood Dream roller coaster and the water ride themed after Jurassic Park will give you an adrenaline boost.

USJ is a hive of entertainment with breathtaking presentations starring your favourite actors from movies like Transformers and Minions. It offers more than just exhilarating rides. Every visit to the park is a special journey because it also celebrates seasonal events.

Judith G. Harrison

Universal Studios Japan is a must-visit location for movie buffs, thrill seekers, and families eager to make memorable moments in the heart of Osaka thanks to its compelling blend of entertainment and imagination.

To get to Universal Studios Japan, you have several transportation options. The most convenient is by train, with a 13-minute ride from *Osaka Station City* costing approximately $1.70 for adults and $0.85 for children. Buses are also available, taking about 30 minutes and costing around $2.70 for adults and $1.40 for children. If you prefer driving, the parking fee is

Judith G Harrison

$23.00 for the day. From Kansai Airport, take a train to Osaka Station City and then transfer to the JR Yumesaki Line, costing about $20.00 for adults and $10.00 for children. Tips include buying tickets in advance, arriving early, using the Universal Express Pass, and taking advantage of free shuttle buses to nearby hotels in Osaka.

Universal Studios Japan ticket prices vary by date and ticket type. As of September 5, 2023, a 1-day ticket costs approximately $65 for adults, $40 for children, and $53 for seniors. Multi-day tickets offer slight discounts per day, with a 2-day adult ticket priced at around $115. It's recommended to buy tickets online for potential savings and consider money-saving strategies such as purchasing in advance, visiting during the off-season, opting for multi-day tickets, or using discount codes.

Judith G Harrison

Osaka Aquarium Kaiyukan

An immersive and informative experience can be had at Osaka Aquarium Kaiyukan, a marine wonderland that lures tourists into the depths of the ocean. It is one of the biggest and most well-known public aquariums in the world and is situated in the thriving Tempozan Harbour Village, making it a must-see sight in Osaka.

This architectural wonder features a massive centre tank that mimics the ecosystem of the Pacific Ocean and is home to a variety of

Judith G Harrison

breathtaking marine creatures, such as whale sharks, manta rays, and vivid schools of fish. You'll come across fascinating exhibits that reflect various aquatic habitats, from the cold Antarctic to the steamy Amazon Rainforest, as you weave your way along its spiral pathways.

In addition to offering a glimpse into the fascinating world below the seas, Osaka Aquarium Kaiyukan also promotes awareness of marine conservation. It is a place that tourists of all ages can enjoy and learn from, making it the ideal addition to any agenda for Osaka.

To get to Universal Studios Japan, you have several transportation options. The most convenient is by train, with a 13-minute ride from Osaka Station City costing approximately $1.70 for adults and $0.85 for children. Buses are also available, taking about 30 minutes and costing around $2.70 for adults and $1.40 for children. If you prefer driving, the parking fee is $23.00 for the day. From Kansai Airport, take a train to Osaka Station City and then transfer to the JR Yumesaki Line, costing about $20.00 for adults and $10.00 for children. Tips include buying tickets in advance, arriving early, using the Universal Express Pass, and taking advantage of free shuttle buses to nearby hotels in Osaka.

Universal Studios Japan ticket prices vary by date and ticket type. A 1-day ticket costs approximately $65 for adults, $40 for children, and $53 for seniors. Multi-day tickets offer slight discounts per day, with a 2-day adult ticket priced at around $115. It's recommended to buy tickets online for potential savings and consider money-saving strategies such as purchasing in advance, visiting during the off-season, opting for multi-day tickets, or using discount codes.

Judith G Harrison

Sumiyoshi Taisha Shrine

In the southern suburbs of Osaka, Sumiyoshi Taisha Shrine is a revered landmark that draws visitors with its timeless beauty and serene environment. It is one of Japan's oldest Shinto temples, dating back more than 1,800 years, and is rich in both historical and cultural value.

The remarkable architectural design of Sumiyoshi Taisha, with its curved bridges and bright vermilion-colored houses, is what makes it stand out. The relationship between the shrine and the sea is reflected in these architectural features, which stand for protection, wealth, and risk-free travel.

Judith G Harrison

Visitors can stroll through the peaceful grounds, over the Taiko Bridge, and take in the quiet atmosphere. The shrine is especially alluring during the annual Shinto festivals and New Year celebrations, when it comes to life with colourful rites and ancient ceremonies.

Inviting visitors to immerse themselves in the essence of Japanese spirituality, Sumiyoshi Taisha Shrine provides a tranquil respite from the busy city of Osaka while upholding a strong link to the country's cultural history.

practical information on how to get to Sumiyoshi Taisha Shrine in

By train: The nearest train station to Sumiyoshi Taisha Shrine is **_Sumiyoshi Station_** on the Osaka Metro Sennichimae Line. The station is about a 5-minute walk from the shrine. The fare is 240 yen (~$2.20) for a single journey.

By bus: There are several buses that stop near Sumiyoshi Taisha Shrine. The most convenient bus stop is Sumiyoshi Taisha-mae, which is about a 1-minute walk from the shrine. The fare is 230 yen (~$2.10) for a single journey.

By taxi: A taxi from Umeda Station to Sumiyoshi Taisha Shrine will cost around 1,500 yen (~$13.50).

The shrine is open from 6:00 AM to 5:00 PM, daily. There is no admission fee.

Judith G Harrison

More tips for visiting Sumiyoshi Taisha Shrine:

- Wear modest clothing that covers your shoulders and knees.
- Remove your shoes before entering the shrine.
- Be respectful of the shrine and its visitors.
- Take your time to appreciate the shrine's architecture and history.

Tsutenkaku Tower

Tsutenkaku, literally "Tower Reaching Heaven," is a tower that rises tall and high in the centre of Osaka, symbolising the tenacity and spirit of the community. This famous monument, which was restored in 1956 after being built in 1912, has come to represent Osaka's post-World War II renaissance.

Tsutenkaku, which rises to a height of 103 metres, provides spectacular panoramic views of the bustling metropolis below. Its peculiar style blends aspects of Japanese and Western architecture to create a singular mix that captures the eclecticism of Osaka.

Additionally, the tower has developed into a cherished gathering spot and a focus of local pride. Shinsekai, a thriving neighbourhood renowned for its unique street cuisine and

Judith G Harrison

nostalgic charm, can be found at its base. For both inhabitants and visitors, Tsutenkaku is a must-visit location where you can take great photos and take in the vivid mood of the city thanks to its lit presence at night.

practical *information* *on* *how* *to* *get* *to* *Tsutenkaku Tower,*

By Train: The nearest train station to Tsutenkaku Tower is Shinsekai Station on the Osaka Metro Midosuji Line. The fare is 250 yen (US$2.25) from Umeda Station. From

Shinsekai Station, it is a 5-minute walk to the tower.

By bus: There are several bus routes that stop near Tsutenkaku Tower. The fare is 230 yen (US$2.00) from Umeda Station.

By Foot: Tsutenkaku Tower is located in the Shinsekai district of Osaka, which is about a 20-minute walk from Umeda Station.

Once you arrive at Tsutenkaku Tower, you can purchase a ticket to enter the tower. The ticket price is 800 yen (US$7.00) for adults and 400 yen (US$3.50) for children.

The tower is open from 9:00am to 10:00pm, but the last entry is at 9:30pm.

Judith G Harrison

Minoo Park and Waterfall

The tranquil refuge of Minoo Park, a haven for both nature lovers and urban escapists, is tucked away just outside of busy Osaka. The mesmerising Minoo Waterfall, a 33-meter waterfall that cascades softly into the Minoo River, is located at the centre of this lovely park.

A trip to Minoo Park provides a lovely diversion from the bustle of the city. You'll be surrounded by lush vegetation, colourful

Judith G Harrison

foliage, and the peaceful sounds of nature as you stroll along the picturesque trails that lead to the waterfall. When the leaves are dressed in their fiery hues in the autumn, it is an especially charming location.

In addition to the waterfall, Minoo Park offers opportunities to see local animals, including the renowned Japanese macaques, as well as attractive temples and tiny shops selling delectable treats like fried maple leaf tempura. Minoo Park and its captivating waterfall provide a refreshing refuge in the middle of Osaka, whether you're hiking, having a picnic, or just taking in the tranquil atmosphere.

Information About Minoo Park and Waterfall,

By train: The closest train station to Minoo Park and Waterfall is Minoo Station on the Hankyu Takarazuka Line. The journey from

Judith G Harrison

Osaka City takes about 30 minutes and costs 350 yen (~$3.20). From Minoo Station, it is a short walk to the park entrance.

By bus: There are also buses that run from Osaka City to Minoo Park and Waterfall. The journey takes about 45 minutes and costs 400 yen (~$3.60). The bus stop is located right in front of the park entrance.

By car: If you are driving, it will take you about an hour from Osaka City to Minoo Park and Waterfall. The park has a free parking lot with space for about 500 cars.

The park is open 24 hours a day, 7 days a week. The entrance fee is 500 yen (~$4.40) for adults and 300 yen (~$2.80) for children.

Here are some more tips for visiting Minoo Park and Waterfall:

Judith G Harrison

- The best time to visit is during the fall foliage season (November to December).
- There are several hiking trails in the park, ranging from easy to challenging.
- There are also several temples and shrines in the park.
- The park is a popular spot for picnicking and camping.

Osaka Museum Of History

A timeless journey through the city's past may be found in the Osaka Museum of History.
The Osaka Museum of History, perched spectacularly atop the Nishinomaru Garden in Osaka Castle Park, provides an enthralling glimpse into the city's colourful past. This

Judith G Harrison

architectural wonder, which resembles a contemporary ark, is a landmark for both history buffs and curious tourists.

The museum's panoramic observation decks offer stunning views of Osaka's skyline and serve as the starting point for a historical trip. A wealth of artefacts, displays, and multimedia presentations inside tell the story of Osaka's development from a feudal stronghold to an industrial powerhouse. Investigate the centuries-long changes in urban architecture, transportation, and daily living.

Judith G Harrison

The Osaka Museum of History is a tribute to the city's rich legacy, inviting visitors to travel back in time and develop a profound understanding of Osaka's significance in moulding Japan's history. It features interactive exhibits, captivating narrative, and a superb location.

Umeda Sky Building

A prime example of contemporary architecture and a symbol of Osaka's forward-thinking nature is the Umeda Sky Building. At the top of this famous twin-tower building is a stunning 'Floating Garden Observatory'. Views of Osaka's expansive cityscape, with its dazzling skyline and urban landscapes extending as far as the eye can reach, are panoramic from this location.

Judith G Harrison

The Umeda Sky Building not only features breathtaking views, but also an immersive experience thanks to its cutting-edge design and engaging exhibitions. The open-air observation deck offers breathtaking sunset views, while the basement level features a recreation of a street from the Showa era, providing a window into Osaka's past.

The Umeda Sky Building is a work of art that promises both aesthetic delight and a distinctive cultural experience, whether you're a traveller wishing for a bird's-eye view of Osaka, a photography enthusiast looking for a

Judith G Harrison

remarkable photo opportunity, a romantic couple seeking a memorable date place, or simply a traveller.

CHAPTER 4: ACCOMMODATIONS OPTIONS

Budget friendly hostel

HOTEL DIAMOND:

- Plain rooms in a straightforward budget hotel with a sitting area & a communal kitchen.

- **Rates** from $26.

- **Location**: 1 Chome-13-21 Taishi, Osaka.

- **Amenities**: communal kitchen, sitting area, free WiFi.

- **Guest rating:** 3.0/5 (based on 395 reviews).

HOTEL GRACERY OSAKA.

- This hotel is located in the Umeda district of Osaka, and it offers rooms with private bathrooms. The hotel also has a number of amenities, including a fitness center and a business center.

- **Price**: Starts at $50 per night

- **Address**: 1-1-8 Umeda, Kita-ku, Osaka, 530-0001, Japan

Judith G Harrison

- **Amenities**: Private bathroom, fitness centre, business centre

HOTEL GRANVIA OSAKA.

- This hotel is located in the Umeda district of Osaka, and it offers rooms with private bathrooms. The hotel also has a number of amenities, including a fitness center, a business center, and a bar.
- **Price**: Starts at $64 per night
- **Address**: 1-1-5 Umeda, Kita-ku, Osaka, 530-0001, Japan
- **Amenities**: Private bathroom, fitness centre, business centre, bar, breakfast buffet

APA HOTEL OSAKA UMEDA EAST.

Judith G Harrison

- This hotel is also located in the Umeda district, and it offers rooms with private bathrooms. The hotel also has a number of amenities, including a coin-operated laundry and a free breakfast buffet.
- **Price**: Starts at $80 per night
- **Address**: 1-3-5 Umeda, Kita-ku, Osaka, 530-0001, Japan
- **Amenities:** Private bathroom, coin-operated laundry, free breakfast buffet

RIHGA ROYAL HOTEL OSAKA.

Judith G Harrison

- This hotel is located in a convenient hub for enjoying Umeda, Namba, Universal Studios Japan and other Osaka attractions, as well as sightseeing in Kyoto. It's a favorite of both locals and tourists throughout its history.
- **Price**: Starts at $100 per night
- **Address**: 1-8-1 Nishi-Umeda, Kita-ku, Osaka, 530-0001, Japan
- **Amenities**: Private bathroom, fitness centre, business centre, bar, breakfast buffet, room service, laundry service

Mid-Range hotels

HOTEL MONTEREY LE PARC OSAKA NAMBA.

- This hotel is located in the Namba district of Osaka, and it offers rooms with private bathrooms. The hotel also has a number of amenities, including a fitness centre, a business centre, and a rooftop bar with views of the city.

- **Price**: Starts at $120 per night
- **Address:** 3-3-30 Nishi-Namba, Chuo-ku, **Osaka**, 542-0076, Japan
- **Amenities:** Private bathroom, fitness centre, business center, rooftop bar with city views, breakfast buffet

HOTEL GRANVIA OSAKA.

- This hotel is located in the Umeda district of Osaka, and it is a popular choice for business travelers. The hotel offers rooms with private bathrooms, as well as a number of amenities, including a fitness center, a business center, and a spa.

- **Price**: Starts at $150 per night
- **Address:** 1-1-3 Umeda, Kita-ku, Osaka, 530-0001, Japan
- **Amenities**: Private bathroom, fitness centre, business centre, spa, breakfast buffet

OSAKA MARRIOTT MIYAKO HOTEL.

- This hotel is located in the Shinsaibashi district of Osaka, and it is a popular choice for couples. The hotel offers rooms with private bathrooms, as well as a number of amenities, including a fitness centre, a spa, and a rooftop bar with views of the city.
- **Price**: Starts at $200 per night

- **Address**: 1-1-33 Nishishinsaibashi, Chuo-ku, Osaka, 542-0081, Japan
- **Amenities**: Private bathroom, fitness centre, spa, rooftop bar with city views, breakfast buffet

RENAISSANCE OSAKA HOTEL.

- This hotel is located in the Umeda district of Osaka, and it is a popular choice for families. The hotel offers rooms with private bathrooms, as well as a number of amenities, including a fitness center, a kids' club, and a game room.
- **Price**: Starts at $120 per night
- **Address**: 1-6-50 Umeda, Kita-ku, Osaka, 530-0001, Japan
- **Amenities**: Private bathroom, fitness centre, kids' club, game room, breakfast buffet

COURTYARD BY MARRIOTT OSAKA SHIN UMEDA.

- This hotel is located in the Umeda district of Osaka, and it is a popular choice for business and leisure travelers. The hotel offers rooms with private bathrooms, as well as a number of amenities, including a fitness center, a business center, and a 24-hour convenience store.
- **Price**: Starts at $150 per night
- **Address**: 1-5-1 Shin Umeda, Kita-ku, Osaka, 530-0001, Japan

Judith G Harrison

- **Amenities**: Private bathroom, fitness center, business center, 24-hour convenience store, breakfast buffet

Luxury hotels

HOTEL GRANVIA OSAKA.

- This hotel is located in the Umeda district of Osaka, and it offers rooms with private bathrooms, a fitness center, and a business center. It also has a number of restaurants and bars.
- Price: Starts at $250 per night
- *Address*: 1-1-3 Umeda, Kita-ku, Osaka, 530-0001, Japan
- *Amenities*: Private bathroom, fitness centre, business centre, restaurants, bars

RENAISSANCE OSAKA HOTEL.

- This hotel is also located in the Umeda district, and it offers similar amenities to Hotel Granvia Osaka. It also has a rooftop bar with views of the city.
- **Price**: Starts at $300 per night
- **Address**: 3-3-4 Umeda, Kita-ku, Osaka, 530-0001, Japan
- **Amenities**: Private bathroom, fitness centre, business centre, restaurants, bars, rooftop bar with city views

HOTEL MONTEREY INTERNATIONAL OSAKA.

- This hotel is located in the Dotombori district of Osaka, and it offers rooms with private bathrooms, a spa, and a sauna. It also has a number of restaurants and bars.
- **Price**: Starts at $350 per night
- **Address**: 1-8-2 Dotombori, Chuo-ku, Osaka, 542-0071, Japan
- **Amenities**: Private bathroom, spa, sauna, restaurants, bars

LE MÉRIDIEN OSAKA:

- This hotel is located in the Shinsaibashi district of Osaka, and it offers rooms with private bathrooms, a fitness center, and a rooftop pool with views of the city.
- **Price**: Starts at $400 per night
- **Address**: 3-3-38 Nishishinsaibashi, Chuo-ku, Osaka, 542-0083, Japan

Judith G Harrison

- **Amenities**: Private bathroom, fitness centre, rooftop pool with city views, restaurants, bars

ROYAL PARK HOTEL OSAKA.

- This hotel is located in the Umeda district, and it is one of the most luxurious hotels in Osaka. It offers rooms with private bathrooms, a spa, a sauna, and a golf course.
- **Price**: Starts at $500 per night
- **Address**: 1-1-4 Umeda, Kita-ku, Osaka, 530-0001, Japan
- **Amenities**: Private bathroom, spa, sauna, golf course, restaurants, bars

Judith G Harrison

CHAPTER 5:

EXPLORING OSAKA'S FOOD SCENES

Introduction to Osaka's Food Culture

The culinary experience of discovering Osaka's cuisine culture is waiting for you. This bustling city, often known as "Japan's Kitchen," is famed for its varied and delicious cuisine. Osaka's cuisine scene offers something for every taste, from takoyaki and okonomiyaki stands on the sidewalk to refined kaiseki dining experiences.

Must-try local specialties that highlight Osaka's distinctive flavours include negiyaki (green onion pancakes) and kitsune udon (udon noodles with sweet tofu). The izakayas (Japanese taverns) in the city provide a glimpse into everyday life, and the busy Kuromon Ichiba Market offers a sensory extravaganza of seasonal produce, seafood, and street food.

Get ready to go on a gastronomic adventure through the diverse food culture of Osaka, where every meal is an exciting new experience.

must-try dishes

1.OKONOMIYAKI:

- This is a savoury pancake made with flour, eggs, cabbage, and other ingredients. It is often topped with mayonnaise, okonomiyaki sauce, and aonori (seaweed).

Judith G Harrison

2.KUSHIKATSU:

- These are skewered and deep-fried pieces of meat, seafood, and vegetables. They are often dipped in a sweet and savoury sauce.

3.TAKOYAKI:

Judith G Harrison

- These are small, ball-shaped dumplings made with octopus, flour, eggs, and other ingredients. They are often topped with mayonnaise, takoyaki sauce, and aonori (seaweed).

4.UDON:

- This is a thick noodle soup made with udon noodles, dashi broth, and other ingredients. It can be topped with a variety of toppings, such as tempura, seafood, or vegetables.

5.SUSHI:

- This is a Japanese dish of vinegared rice topped with seafood, vegetables, or other ingredients. There are many different types of sushi, so you can find something to suit your taste.

6.RAMEN:

- This is a Japanese noodle soup made with ramen noodles, dashi broth, and other ingredients. It can be topped with a variety of toppings, such as pork, chicken, or vegetables.

7.KAISEKI:

- This is a multi-course Japanese meal that typically consists of small, delicate dishes. Each dish is carefully prepared and presented, and the meal is meant to be an experience of both taste and visual beauty.

Judith G Harrison

8.DANGO:

- These are small, glutinous rice dumplings that are often served on skewers. They can be plain or flavored with different ingredients, such as sweet bean paste or kinako (roasted soybean flour).

9.HORUMONYAKI:

- This is a dish of grilled offal, such as intestines, stomach, and tripe. It is often served with a dipping sauce made with soy sauce, mirin, and sake.

10.TSUKEMEN:

Judith G Harrison

- This is a noodle dish in which the noodles are dipped in a separate dipping sauce. The dipping sauce is typically made with soy sauce, vinegar, and other ingredients.

11.CURRY NANBAN MESHI:

- This is a dish of rice topped with curry and chicken that has been coated in a tempura batter and deep-fried.

12.KITSUNE UDON:

- This is a bowl of udon noodles topped with aburaage (fried tofu).

Judith G Harrison

13.MONJAYAKI:

- This is a savory pancake similar to okonomiyaki, but it is made with a different batter and is often topped with different ingredients, such as cheese, corn, and vegetables.

14.FUGU:

- This is a dish of blowfish, which is a poisonous fish. Fugu is prepared by specially trained chefs who know how to remove the poisonous parts of the fish.

15.TEPPANYAKI:

- This is a dish of meat, seafood, or vegetables that is cooked on a hot plate in front of the diners.

Judith G Harrison

16.NATTO:

- This is a fermented soybean dish that has a strong smell and taste. Natto is often eaten with rice and other toppings, such as mustard or soy sauce.

TOP RESTAURANTS AND IZAKAYAS

Here are some of the top restaurants and izakayas in Osaka and their addresses:

OKONOMIYAKI KIJIYA: This is a famous okonomiyaki restaurant located in the Shinsekai district. It is known for its delicious and generous portions of okonomiyaki.

- Address: 2-8-1 Dotombori, Chuo-ku, Osaka, 542-0071, Japan
- Hours: 11:30 AM - 11:00 PM

IZAKAYA UMEDA NOWA:

- This is a popular izakaya located in the Umeda district. It is known for its wide variety of Japanese dishes, including sake, beer, and yakitori.

- Address: 1-1-1 Umeda, Kita-ku, Osaka, 530-0001, Japan
- Hours: 5:00 PM - 11:00 PM

SHINSAIBASHI TSURUKAME:

- This is a popular sushi restaurant located in the Shinsaibashi district. It is known for its fresh and delicious sushi.
- **Address**: 1-7-12 Shinsaibashi, Chuo-ku, Osaka, 542-0081, Japan
- **Hours**: 11:30 AM - 11:00 PM

HANAMARU SOBA:

- This is a popular soba restaurant located in the Dotonbori district. It is known for its delicious and affordable soba.

Judith G Harrison

- **Address**: 2-10-10 Dotombori, Chuo-ku, Osaka, 542-0071, Japan
- **Hours**: 11:30 AM - 9:00 PM

Themed Dining Experiences

Here are 5 themed dining experiences in Osaka, Japan.

1. Kushikatsu Daruma:

- A conveyor belt sushi restaurant where you cook your own skewered meat and vegetables at your table.

Judith G Harrison

- **Address:** 1-3-3 Nishitenma, Kita-ku, Osaka-shi, Osaka Prefecture 530-0047, Japan
- **Phone**: +81 6-6363-5544
- **Opening hours:** 11:30am-11pm
- **Price range:** ¥1,000-¥2,000 (US$10-US$20)

2. Kappou Okamoto:

- A traditional Japanese counter restaurant where you can watch the chef prepare your meal right in front of you.
- **Address:** 2-1-18 Dotombori, Chuo-ku, Osaka-shi, Osaka Prefecture 542-0071, Japan

- **Phone**: +81 6-6211-3888
- **Opening hours:** 11:30am-2pm, 5pm-9:30pm
- **Price range:** ¥2,000-¥3,000 (US$20-US$30)

Judith G Harrison

3. Sushi Kimura:

- A Michelin-starred sushi restaurant where you can enjoy the freshest, highest quality sushi.
- **Address**: 1-1-2 Nishishinsaibashi, Chuo-ku, Osaka-shi, Osaka Prefecture 542-0085, Japan
- **Phone:** +81 6-6226-2550
- **Opening hours:** 6pm-11pm (closed on Wednesdays)
- **Price range:** ¥3,000-¥5,000 (US$30-US$50)

4. Okonomiyaki Mizuno:

- A popular restaurant that serves Osaka-style okonomiyaki, a savory pancake made with cabbage, eggs, and other ingredients.

- **Address:** 3-3-12 Dotombori, Chuo-ku, Osaka-shi, Osaka Prefecture 542-0071, Japan
- **Phone**: +81 6-6211-1626
- **Opening hours:** 11am-11pm
- **Price range:** ¥1,500-¥2,000 (US$15-US$20)

5. Kuromon Ichiba

- A large, covered market where you can buy fresh seafood, meat, vegetables, and other food items. There are also many restaurants in the market where you can try the food you buy.

Judith G Harrison

- **Address:** 1-1 Kuromon, Chuo-ku, Osaka-shi, Osaka Prefecture 542-0071, Japan
- **Opening hours:** 9am-6pm (closed on Sunday

Vegetarian and Dietary Options

Here are 5 vegetarian restaurants in Osaka, Japan.

1.GREEN EARTH

- **Address**: 4-2-2 Kitakyuhojimachi, Chuo-ku, Osaka-shi, Osaka Prefecture 540-0004, Japan
- **Phone**: +81 6-6251-1245
- **Opening hours:** 11:30am-4pm (closed on Mondays)
- **Price range:** ¥1,000-¥2,000 (US$10-US$20)

Judith G Harrison

- Vegetarian and vegan options
- English menu available

This restaurant has been serving vegetarian food since 1991 and is a popular spot for both locals and tourists. The menu features a variety of Japanese and Western dishes, all made with fresh, seasonal ingredients.

2. PAPRIKA SHOKUDO VEGAN:

- **Address:** 1-9-9 Shinmachi, Chuo-ku, Osaka-shi, Osaka Prefecture 542-0081, Japan
- **Phone:** +81 6-6599-9788
- **Opening hours:** 11:30am-2pm, 5:30pm-9pm (closed on Tuesdays)

* Price range: ¥1,000-¥2,000 (US$10-US$20)

- Vegan options
- English menu available

This restaurant serves modern Japanese cuisine with a vegan twist. The menu features dishes like vegan ramen, curry, and udon.

3. Shama Vegetarian Indian Restaurant:

- **Address**: 1-3-7 Kitahorie, Chuo-ku, Osaka-shi, Osaka Prefecture 541-0044, Japan
- **Phone**: +81 6-6536-6669
- Opening hours: 11am-3pm, 5pm-10pm (closed on Mondays)
- **Price range:** ¥1,000-¥1,500 (US$10-US$15)
- Indian food
- English menu available

This restaurant serves authentic Indian cuisine, all of which is vegetarian. The menu features a variety of dishes, including tandoori, curry, and biryani.

Judith G Harrison

4. Genmai Cafe:

- **Address:** 1-1-8 Dotombori, Chuo-ku, Osaka-shi, Osaka Prefecture 542-0071, Japan
- **Phone:** +81 6-6212-6821
- **Opening hours:** 11am-10pm
- **Price range:** ¥700-¥1,000 (US$7-US$10)
- Vegetarian and vegan options
- No English menu

This cafe is a popular spot for both locals and tourists. It serves a variety of healthy and vegetarian dishes, such as brown rice bowls, salads, and smoothies.

5. Tenshin:

- **Address:** 1-9-12 Nishitenma, Kita-ku, Osaka-shi, Osaka Prefecture 530-0047, Japan
- **Phone**: +81 6-6363-0033
- **Opening hours:** 11:30am-2:30pm, 5:30pm-9pm (closed on Tuesdays)
- **Price range:** ¥1,500-¥2,000 (US$15-US$20)
- Japanese cuisine
- No English menu

This restaurant serves traditional Japanese cuisine, all of which is vegetarian. The menu

Judith G Harrison

features a variety of dishes, including tempura, udon, and sushi.

Here are some other things to keep in mind when looking for vegetarian and dietary options in Osaka:

- Many Japanese restaurants offer a vegetarian or vegan option, even if it is not specifically advertised.
- It is always a good idea to ask the waiter or waitress if there are any vegetarian or dietary options available.
- There are also many vegan and vegetarian grocery stores in Osaka where you can buy ingredients to cook your own meals.

Judith G Harrison

CHAPTER 5: SHOPPING IN OSAKA

Shopping Districts and Streets

Some of the most popular shopping districts and streets in Osaka, with average expenses includs

DOTONBORI: This is the most famous shopping district in Osaka. It is known for its neon lights, restaurants, and bars. The average expense per day in Dotonbori is around $50.

Judith G Harrison

SHINSAIBASHI: This is another popular shopping district in Osaka. It is home to many department stores, boutiques, and arcades. The average expense per day in Shinsaibashi is around $40.

UMEDA: This is the largest commercial district in Osaka. It is home to many office buildings, hotels, and shopping malls. The average expense per day in Umeda is around $30.

TENJINBASHISUJI SHOPPING ARCADE: This is the longest covered shopping arcade in Japan. It is home to over 2,000 stores selling a variety of goods. The average expense per day in Tenjinbashisuji Shopping Arcade is around $20.

Judith G Harrison

SENNICHIMAE SHOTENGAI: This is a traditional shopping street in Osaka. It is home to many small shops selling a variety of goods. The average expense per day in Sennichimae Shotengai is around $15.

Traditional Markets

Here are some of the most popular traditional markets in Osaka and their locations:

Judith G Harrison

KUROMON ICHIBA MARKET: This is the largest and most famous market in Osaka. It is located in the Shinsaibashi district and is a great place to buy fresh seafood, produce, and other food items.

TENJINBASHISUJI KŌJŌ MARKET: This is the longest covered market in Japan. It is located in the Umeda district and is a great place to buy clothes, household goods, and other items.

NAMBA MARKET: This is a lively market located in the Namba district. It is a great place to buy souvenirs, snacks, and other items.

SHINSEKAI MARKET: This is a traditional market located in the Shinsekai district. It is a great place to buy food, souvenirs, and other items.

Judith G Harrison

SENNICHIMASHI   SHOTENGAI MARKET: This is a traditional shopping street located in the Dotonbori district. It is a great place to buy souvenirs, snacks, and other items.

Modern Shopping Malls

Here are some of the modern shopping malls in Osaka with average expenses:

GRAND FRONT OSAKA: This is a large, modern shopping mall located in the Umeda district. It is home to over 200 stores, including department stores, boutiques, and restaurants. The average expense per day in Grand Front Osaka is around $50.

Judith G Harrison

HEP FIVE: This is a popular shopping mall located in the Shinsaibashi district. It is home to over 150 stores, including fashion brands, cosmetics stores, and electronics stores. The average expense per day in HEP FIVE is around $40.

LUCUA OSAKA: This is a large, modern shopping mall located in the Umeda district. It is home to over 200 stores, including department stores, boutiques, and restaurants. The average expense per day in LUCUA Osaka is around $30.

TENJINBASHISUJI   PREMIUM OUTLETS: This is an outlet mall located in the Tenjinbashisuji district. It is home to over 100 stores selling discounted designer brands. The average expense per day in Tenjinbashisuji Premium Outlets is around $20.

Judith G Harrison

NAMBA PARKS: This is a large, modern shopping mall located in the Namba district. It is home to over 200 stores, including department stores, boutiques, and restaurants. The average expense per day in Namba Parks is around $15.

These are just a few of the many modern shopping malls in Osaka. The actual expenses may vary depending on the stores you visit and your spending habits.

Souvenir and Gift Ideas

Here are some souvenir and gift ideas in Osaka:

OKONOMIYAKI AND TAKOYAKI PANS:
These are the pans used to make okonomiyaki and takoyaki, two of Osaka's most famous dishes. They make great souvenirs for people who love to cook or who are interested in Japanese culture.

DANGO: These are small, glutinous rice dumplings that are often served on skewers. They can be a sweet or savory snack, and they make great souvenirs for people who love Japanese food.

SUMO WRESTLER DOLLS: Sumo is a traditional Japanese sport, and sumo wrestler dolls are popular souvenirs. They come in all shapes and sizes, and they make great gifts for children and adults alike.

Judith G Harrison

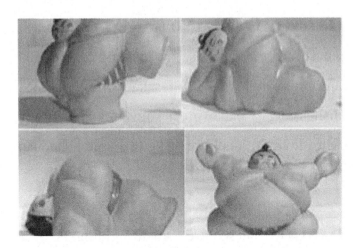

HANDMADE CRAFTS: Osaka is home to many talented artisans, and there are many beautiful handmade crafts available as souvenirs. These include ceramics, textiles, and woodwork.

FOOD PRODUCTS: Osaka is known for its delicious food, and there are many food products available as souvenirs. These include spices, sauces, and snacks.

TRADITIONAL CLOTHING: Kimono and yukata are traditional Japanese clothing. They

Judith G Harrison

make great souvenirs for people who want to experience Japanese culture or who want to wear something unique.

These are just a few ideas for souvenirs and gifts you can buy in Osaka. The best souvenir is something that is meaningful to you or the person you are giving it to.

More souvenir and gift ideas in Osaka:

T-shirts and other clothing with Osaka-related prints:

Judith G Harrison

- This is a popular choice for souvenirs because it is both practical and affordable. You can find t-shirts, hoodies, bags, and other items with prints of Osaka landmarks, food, or culture.

KEYCHAINS AND OTHER SMALL SOUVENIRS:

- These are also popular souvenirs because they are easy to pack and carry. You can find keychains with the Osaka city logo, or with other symbols of Osaka, such as takoyaki or okonomiyaki.

TRADITIONAL JAPANESE SWEETS:

- These are delicious and unique souvenirs that people from all over the world enjoy. You can find a variety of traditional Japanese sweets in Osaka, such as mochi, wagashi, and dango.

OSAKA SAKE:

- Osaka is known for its sake, so this is a great souvenir for people who enjoy Japanese alcohol. You can find a variety of sake brands and varieties in Osaka, so you're sure to find one that the recipient will enjoy.

BOOKS AND MAGAZINES ABOUT OSAKA:

- This is a great souvenir for people who want to learn more about Osaka. You can find books and magazines about Osaka history, culture, and food.

Bargaining Tips

Here are some bargaining tips when shopping in Osaka:

Judith G Harrison

Be confident: The first step to bargaining is to be confident. If you seem unsure of yourself, the shopkeeper is less likely to negotiate with you.

Do your research: Before you start bargaining, it is important to do your research and know the approximate value of the item you are interested in. This will help you avoid overpaying.

Start Low: When you start bargaining, it is always best to start low. This gives you room to negotiate and come to a mutually agreeable price.

Be willing to walk away: If you are not happy with the price, be willing to walk away. This shows the shopkeeper that you are serious about getting a good deal.

Judith G Harrison

Be Friendly And Polite: Even though you are bargaining, it is important to be friendly and polite to the shopkeeper. This will help create a good atmosphere and make the bargaining process more enjoyable.

Understand The Culture: Bargaining is a common practice in Osaka, but it is important to understand the cultural nuances. For example, it is considered rude to bargain too aggressively or to haggle over small amounts of money.

Here are some additional tips:

Bargain in Japanese: If you can speak Japanese, bargaining in Japanese will make you seem more confident and serious to the shopkeeper.

Use body language: Body language can be a powerful tool when bargaining. Make eye

Judith G Harrison

contact, smile, and nod your head to show that you are interested in the item and that you are willing to negotiate.

Be Patient: Bargaining can take time, so be patient and don't get discouraged if you don't get the price you want right away.

CHAPTER 6: NIGHTLIFE AND ENTERTAINMENT

Osaka's Vibrant Nightlife

Osaka's nightlife is a pulsating symphony of lights, laughter, and boundless energy. As the sun sets, the city transforms into a neon-lit wonderland, offering an electrifying array of entertainment. From the bustling streets of

Dotonbori, where iconic billboards compete for attention, to the atmospheric bars tucked away in Nakazakicho, every corner beckons with its unique charm. Savor local street food delights, dance to eclectic beats in nightclubs, or unwind in izakayas with locals. Osaka's vibrant nightlife knows no bounds, promising unforgettable moments and a taste of the city's vivacious spirit that thrives well into the early hours of the morning.

Judith G Harrison

Bars and Pubs

Here are 5 bars and pubs in Osaka, Japan with their practical information:

1.The Blarney Stone Shinsaibashi: is an Irish pub located in the heart of Shinsaibashi, one of the most popular shopping and nightlife districts in Osaka. It is a popular spot for both tourists and locals, and is known for its friendly atmosphere, wide selection of beers, and live music.

Judith G Harrison

- **Opening hours:** 5pm - 1am (Thursday - Wednesday)
- **Address:** Higashishinsaibashi, 2 Chome−5−27 幸田ビル
- Phone number: +81 6-6484-2220

2. Fiji Bar Osaka: is a sports bar with a rugby theme located in Soemon-cho, a quiet area near Dotonbori. It is a great place to watch a game or just relax with friends and enjoy a drink. The bar has a wide selection of beers on tap, as well as cocktails and bar food.

[Image of Fiji Bar Osaka, Osaka]

- **Opening hours:** 6pm - 11:30pm (Thursday - Sunday); Closed on Monday and Tuesday
- **Address:** Mittera Galaxie building 2-B1-A ,Soemon-cho, 5 Chome-5-30 B1
- **Phone number:** +81 80-3112-5161

Judith G Harrison

3. Bar Nayuta: is a speakeasy-style bar located in Umeda, a major business district in Osaka. It is known for its creative cocktails, which are made with fresh, seasonal ingredients. The bar has a small and intimate atmosphere, making it a great place to have a conversation with friends.

[Image of Bar Nayuta, Osaka]

- **Opening hours:** 6pm - 12am (Thursday - Saturday); Closed on Sunday, Monday, and Tuesday
- **Address:** 1 Chome-1-11 Umeda, Kita Ward, Osaka, 530-0001, Japan
- **Phone number:** +81 6-6373-5588

4. Moon Tower: is a rooftop bar located in Namba, another popular nightlife district in Osaka. It offers stunning views of the city skyline, making it a great place to enjoy a drink and take in the sights. The bar has a wide selection of cocktails, beers, and wines, as well as bar food.

[Image of Moon Tower, Osaka]

- **Opening hours:** 5pm - 11pm (Sunday - Thursday); 5pm - 1am (Friday and Saturday)

Judith G Harrison

- **Address**: 1 Chome-8-30 Dotombori, Chuo Ward, Osaka, 542-0071, Japan
- **Phone number:** +81 6-6212-0100

5. CinqueCento: is a small bar located in Shinsaibashi, known for its affordable drinks and friendly atmosphere. It is a popular spot for both locals and tourists, and is a great place to meet new people. The bar has a wide selection of beers, cocktails, and wines, as well as bar food.

[Image of CinqueCento, Osaka]

- **Opening hours:** 5pm - 1am (Monday - Saturday); Closed on Sunday

Judith G Harrison

- **Address**: 1 Chome-7-12 Nishishinsaibashi, Chuo Ward, Osaka, 542-0071, Japan
- **Phone number:** +81 6-6212-0100

Nightclubs and Live Music Venues

Here are some of the most popular nightclubs and live music venues in Osaka:

OWL OSAKA: This is a large nightclub located in the Umeda district. It is known for its EDM music and its laser light shows.

CIRCUS: This is a small but lively nightclub located in the Dotonbori district. It is known for its house music and its friendly atmosphere.

SAM AND DAVE ONE: This is a live music venue located in the Shinsaibashi district. It is known for its blues and jazz music.

Billboard Live Osaka: This is a large live music venue located in the Umeda district. It is known for its variety of music, including pop, rock, and classical music.

Judith G Harrison

FEVER: This is a large nightclub located in the Namba district. It is known for its hip hop music and its dance parties.

CHAPTER 7: OUTDOOR AND RECREATIONAL ACTIVITIES

Parks and Gardens

Osaka Castle Park: This is the most famous park in Osaka. It is located in the center of the city and is home to Osaka Castle, a UNESCO World Heritage Site. The park is open from 9:00 am to 5:00 pm and admission is 600 yen for adults and 300 yen for children.

Judith G Harrison

Namba Parks: This is a large park located in the Namba district. It is home to a variety of gardens, shops, and restaurants. The park is open from 10:00 am to 9:00 pm and admission is free.

Tennoji Park: This is a large park located in the Tennoji district. It is home to a zoo, a botanical garden, and a Japanese garden. The park is open from 9:00 am to 5:00 pm and admission is 500 yen for adults and 300 yen for children.

Judith G Harrison

Shinsekai Garden: This is a small park located in the Shinsekai district. It is home to a variety of flowers and plants. The park is open from 9:00 am to 5:00 pm and admission is free.

Osaka Botanical Garden: This is a large botanical garden located in the Suita city. It is home to a variety of plants from all over the world. The garden is open from 9:00 am to 4:30 pm and admission is 500 yen for adults and 300 yen for children.

Cycling and Walking Tours

There are many cycling and walking tours available in Osaka. Here are a few options:

Judith G Harrison

CYCLE OSAKA: This company offers a variety of cycling tours, including a city tour, a food tour, and a historical tour. The tours range in price from $35 to $55 per person.

OSAKA FOODIE BIKE TOUR: This tour takes you to some of Osaka's best food spots, including takoyaki, okonomiyaki, and kushikatsu. The tour costs $45 per person.

OSAKA CASTLE WALKING TOUR: This tour takes you to Osaka Castle, a UNESCO World Heritage Site. The tour costs $25 per person.

Judith G Harrison

SHINSEKAI GRAFFITI WALL WALKING TOUR:

This tour takes you to the Shinsekai district, where you can see some of Osaka's most famous graffiti walls. The tour costs $20 per person.

NAMBA NAMBA WALKING TOUR: This tour takes you to the Namba district, where you can see some of Osaka's most famous landmarks, such as Dotombori and Namba Parks. The tour costs $20 per person.

**When choosing a cycling or walking tour, it is important to consider the following factors:**

Your fitness level: If you are not a regular cyclist or walker, you may want to choose a tour that is shorter or less strenuous.

Judith G Harrison

ormat...

132

Your interests: There are tours that focus on different aspects of Osaka, such as food, history, or culture. Choose a tour that interests you the most.

Your budget: Tours can range in price from very affordable to quite expensive. Set a budget before you start looking at tours.

Onsen (Hot Springs) Experiences

Some of the best onsen experiences in Osaka:

Solaniwa Onsen Osaka Bay Tower: is a large onsen complex located in the heart of Osaka. It

Judith G Harrison

has a variety of hot spring baths, including indoor, outdoor, and open-air baths. There are also a swimming pool, a sauna, and a restaurant.

Minoh Onsen Spa Garden: is a traditional onsen located in the mountains of Minoh. It has a variety of hot spring baths, including arotenburo (open-air baths). There is also a garden, a restaurant, and a souvenir shop.

Niji no Yu: is a modern onsen located in the Umeda district of Osaka. It has a variety of hot spring baths, including a rooftop bath with city views. There is also a restaurant and a bar.

Nobeha no Yu Tsuruhashi: is an onsen located in the Tsuruhashi district of Osaka. It is a Korean-style onsen that has a variety of hot spring baths, including arotenburo and a salt scrub.

Kamigata Onsen Ikkyu: is an onsen located near Universal Studios Japan. It has a variety of hot spring baths, including arotenburo and a sauna. There is also a restaurant and a bar.

Here are some additional tips for enjoying an onsen in Osaka:

Be sure to shower before entering the hot spring baths.

- Wear a yukata (a traditional Japanese robe) or a swimsuit.
- Don't forget to bring a towel.
- Be respectful of other guests and follow the onsen's rules.

CHAPTER 8: ITINERARY

3 AND 7 DAYS ITINERARY FOR ADVENTURE SEEKERS

3-day itinerary for adventure seekers in Osaka:

DAY 1:

- **visit osaka castle (天守閣, tenshukaku).** This iconic castle is a must-see for any visitor to Osaka. You can climb to the top of the castle for stunning views of the city.

Judith G Harrison

- **Explore Dotonbori district** (道頓堀). This vibrant district is known for its neon lights, street food, and arcades. Be sure to try some of Osaka's famous dishes, such as takoyaki (octopus balls) and okonomiyaki (a savory pancake).

- **Take a boat tour of Osaka Bay** (大阪湾). This is a great way to see the city from a different perspective and get some fresh air.

DAY 2:

- **Go hiking in Mount Koya** (高野山): This UNESCO World Heritage Site is home to hundreds of temples and shrines. It is a great place to escape the hustle and bustle of the city and experience Japanese nature.

Judith G Harrison

- **Visit Nara Park (奈良公園):** This park is home to over 1,000 deer, which are considered sacred animals in Japan. You can feed and pet the deer, or simply enjoy their company.

- **Take a day trip to Kyoto (京都).** This ancient city is home to many UNESCO World Heritage Sites, such as Kiyomizu-dera Temple and Arashiyama Bamboo Grove.

Day 3:

- **Visit Universal Studios Japan (ユニバーサル・スタジオ・ジャパン).** This theme park is a great place to spend a day if you are looking for some thrills. There are rides based on popular movies and TV shows, such as Harry Potter, Jurassic Park, and Minions.

Judith G Harrison

- **Go shopping in Umeda (梅田):** This area is home to many department stores and shopping malls. You can find everything from souvenirs to high-end fashion here.

- **Enjoy the nightlife in Shinsaibashi (心斎橋).** This district is known for its bars, clubs, and restaurants. It is a great place to let loose and have some fun.

7-day itinerary for adventure seekers in Osaka:

Day 1: Follow the 3-day itinerary above.

DAY 4:

- **Go white-water rafting on the Yodo River (淀川):** This is a great way to experience the adrenaline rush of

Judith G Harrison

white-water rafting in a safe and controlled environment.

- **Visit the Osaka Science Museum (**大阪市科学館**):** This museum has exhibits on a variety of scientific topics, such as space, dinosaurs, and robots.

DAY 5:

- **Take a day trip to Himeji Castle (**姫路城**):** This UNESCO World Heritage Site is known as the "White Heron Castle" due to its elegant white exterior.

- **Visit the Kaiyukan Aquarium (**海遊館**).** This aquarium is home to over 30,000 marine animals, including sharks, dolphins, and penguins.

DAY 6:

Judith G Harrison

- **Go hiking in Yoshinoyama** (吉野山). This mountain range is home to over 3,000 cherry trees, which bloom in springtime.

- **Visit the Dotombori River Walk** (道頓 堀川ウォーク)**:** This is a great place to take a stroll and enjoy the views of the Dotombori district.

Day 7:

- **Relax at a Japanese spa** (温泉)**:** This is a great way to soak away your stress and rejuvenate your body.

Enjoy a farewell meal at a local restaurant. This is a great way to end your trip and sample some more of Osaka's delicious food.

Judith G Harrison

3 AND 7 DAYS ITINERARY FOR FAMILIES

Here's a 3-day itinerary for families visiting Osaka, Japan:

DAY 1:

MORNING:

- **Osaka Castle:** Start your day with a visit to the majestic Osaka Castle. Explore the castle grounds, climb to the top for panoramic views, and learn about its historical significance.

- **akoyaki at Dotonbori:** Head to the lively Dotonbori district for lunch. Try Osaka's famous street food, takoyaki (octopus balls), from one of the many vendors.

AFTERNOON:

- **Shitenno-ji Temple:** Discover Japan's oldest Buddhist temple, Shitenno-ji. Explore the serene temple grounds, and take a moment for reflection in the peaceful surroundings.

- **Tennoji Park and Zoo** Nearby, visit Tennoji Park and Zoo. It's a great place for kids to see animals and play in the park.

EVENING:

- **Dotonbori Street:** Return to Dotonbori in the evening to witness the district come alive with neon lights. Stroll along the canal, take photos with the Glico Running Man sign, and enjoy a delicious dinner at one of the many restaurants.

DAY 2: FAMILY-FRIENDLY FUN

MORNING:

- **Universal Studios Japan (Usj):** Spend the day at Universal Studios Japan, located in Osaka. Enjoy thrilling rides, meet beloved characters, and experience the magic of movie-themed attractions.

- **Universal CityWalk:** Grab lunch at Universal CityWalk, filled with a variety of dining options suitable for all tastes.

Judith G Harrison

AFTERNOON:

- **Aquarium Kaiyukan:** After leaving Universal Studios, visit the Osaka Aquarium Kaiyukan, one of the largest and most impressive aquariums in the world. Explore its diverse marine life and interactive exhibits.

EVENING:

- **TEMPOZAN FERRIS WHEEL:** Adjacent to the aquarium is the Tempozan Ferris Wheel. Take a ride for stunning views of Osaka Bay and the city skyline.

DAY 3: CULTURAL AND NATURAL EXPLORATION

MORNING:

- **Kuromon Ichiba Market:** Begin your day at Kuromon Ichiba Market, known as "Osaka's Kitchen." Sample local street foods and shop for fresh produce and souvenirs.

- **Street Food Adventure:** Embrace the vibrant street food culture of Osaka. Try okonomiyaki (savory pancake) or kushikatsu (skewered and deep-fried delights) at street stalls.

AFTERNOON:

- **Osaka Science Museum**: Head to the Osaka Science Museum for interactive and educational exhibits suitable for all ages. It's a great way to engage children in science and technology.

- **Nakanoshima Park:** Enjoy a leisurely walk in Nakanoshima Park, a beautiful urban oasis with gardens, sculptures, and river views.

EVENING:

- **Nighttime Cruise**: End your family trip with a relaxing nighttime cruise along the Okawa River. It's a magical way to see Osaka's illuminated skyline.

__Here's a 7-day itinerary for families visiting Osaka, Japan.__

DAY 1:

MORNING:

- Arrival in Osaka, check into your accommodation.

AFTERNOON:

- Explore Dotonbori, a bustling entertainment and shopping district.
- Savor street food like takoyaki and okonomiyaki.

EVENING:

- Stroll along the canal and marvel at the neon lights and iconic Glico Running Man sign.

DAY 2:

MORNING:

- Visit Osaka Castle. Explore the castle grounds and enjoy the panoramic view from the top.

AFTERNOON:

- Head to the Osaka Museum of History, which offers interactive exhibits for all ages.

EVENING:

- Relax at your accommodation or explore local dining options.

DAY 3:

FULL DAY:

- Spend the day at Universal Studios Japan. Enjoy thrilling rides, shows, and meet beloved characters.

EVENING:

Judith G Harrison

- Dine at Universal CityWalk Osaka for a variety of culinary options.

DAY 4: NARA DAY TRIP

FULL DAY:

- Take a day trip to Nara. Visit Nara Park to feed and interact with friendly deer.
- Explore Todai-ji Temple and Kasuga Taisha Shrine.

EVENING:

- Return to Osaka and have a relaxing dinner in your chosen neighborhood.

DAY 5: KYOTO DAY TRIP

FULL DAY:

- Take a day trip to Kyoto. Explore the Arashiyama Bamboo Grove, visit Kinkaku-ji (the Golden Pavilion), and wander through Gion.

Judith G Harrison

EVENING:

- Return to Osaka and savor a delicious dinner.

DAY 6: OSAKA AQUARIUM KAIYUKAN AND TEMPOZAN HARBOR VILLAGE.

MORNING:

- Visit Osaka Aquarium Kaiyukan, one of the largest aquariums in the world.

AFTERNOON:

- Explore Tempozan Harbor Village, which includes an entertainment complex, Ferris wheel, and shopping mall.

EVENING:

Judith G Harrison

- Enjoy waterfront dining at one of the harbor's restaurants.

DAY 7: ADVENTURE IN MINOO PARK AND FAREWELL

MORNING:
- Head to Minoo Park for a nature-filled adventure. Hike to Minoo Waterfall and enjoy the beautiful surroundings.

AFTERNOON:
- Return to Osaka and spend your last few hours shopping for souvenirs or relaxing at your favorite spot.

EVENING:
- Bid farewell to Osaka and reflect on your wonderful family adventure.

3 AND 7 DAYS ITINERARY FOR ART ENTHUSIAST

3-day itinerary for art enthusiasts in a city like Osaka,

DAY 1:

MORNING:

- **Osaka Castle**: Start your art journey with a visit to Osaka Castle, an iconic symbol of the city. Explore the castle's museum, which houses historical artifacts and artworks, providing insights into Japan's feudal past.

Judith G Harrison

Lunch:

- Enjoy a traditional Japanese lunch at a local restaurant near Osaka Castle, savoring dishes like sushi or tempura.

AFTERNOON

- **Shitenno-ji Temple:** Head to Shitenno-ji Temple, one of Japan's oldest Buddhist temples. Admire the architecture and serene gardens that inspire contemplation and reflection.

- **Dotonbori:** Dive into the vibrant energy of Dotonbori in the evening. Explore the bustling streets filled with neon signs, street art, and bustling shops. Don't miss the iconic Glico Running Man sign and the whimsical mechanical crab.

Judith G Harrison

DINNER:

- Savor Osaka's renowned street food in
Dotonbori. Try takoyaki (octopus balls),
okonomiyaki (savory pancake), and
kushikatsu (deep-fried skewers) from
local stalls.

<h3 style="text-align:center">DAY 2:</h3>

MORNING:

- Nakanoshima Public Art**: Begin your
day with a visit to Nakanoshima, known
for its public art installations. Explore
the outdoor sculptures and enjoy a
peaceful stroll along the riverbank.

Lunch:

- Have lunch at a trendy café or restaurant
in the Nakanoshima area.

Judith G Harrison

AFTERNOON:

- **National Museum of Art, Osaka (NMAO)**: Dive into contemporary art at the NMAO, home to a remarkable collection of Japanese and international modern art. Explore the ever-changing exhibitions and installations that push the boundaries of creativity.

- **Kuromon Ichiba Market:** After the museum, visit Kuromon Ichiba Market for a sensory experience of local flavors, fresh produce, and street food.

Dinner:

- Head to the lively district of Kitashinchi, where you can enjoy a fine dining experience at a restaurant that combines artistry with cuisine.

Judith G Harrison

DAY 3:

MORNING:

- **Sumiyoshi Taisha Shrine:** Begin your day with a visit to Sumiyoshi Taisha, a unique shrine with picturesque arched bridges and unique architectural features.

Lunch:

- Explore local restaurants near the shrine for a traditional Japanese meal.

AFTERNOON:

- **Abeno Harukas Art Museum:** Discover contemporary Japanese art at the Abeno Harukas Art Museum, located in Japan's tallest building, Abeno Harukas. Enjoy panoramic city views from the observation deck.

Judith G Harrison

- **Shinsaibashi and Amerikamura**: Spend your afternoon exploring the trendy shopping districts of Shinsaibashi and Amerikamura, where you can find boutique stores, street art, and unique fashion.

Dinner:

- For your final dinner in Osaka, indulge in a kaiseki (traditional multi-course) meal at a restaurant that showcases artistry in both presentation and taste.

7-day itinerary for art enthusiasts exploring Osaka, Japan.

DAY 1:

Judith G Harrison

- Arrival: Arrive in Osaka and check-in to your accommodation.
- **Dotonbori Exploration:** Stroll through Dotonbori, a lively district with vibrant street art and illuminated billboards. Discover the iconic Glico Running Man and snap photos of the Dotonbori Canal.

DAY 2:

Nakanoshima: Start your day at Nakanoshima, where you can visit the Osaka Science Museum and the National Museum of Art Osaka.

Lunch: Enjoy a Japanese meal at a local restaurant.

Abeno Harukas Art Museum: Explore the Abeno Harukas Art Museum, located in Japan's tallest building. It hosts various contemporary art exhibitions.

Judith G Harrison

Evening at Umeda Arts Theater: Check out Umeda Arts Theater for theatrical performances and musicals.

DAY 3: HISTORIC AND TRADITIONAL ART

Osaka Castle: Visit Osaka Castle, known for its historical significance and beautiful architecture. Explore the museum within the castle grounds.

Lunch: Try some local Osaka street food.

Shitenno-ji Temple: Head to Shitenno-ji Temple, one of the oldest Buddhist temples in Japan, and explore its serene gardens and architecture.

Judith G Harrison

Tennoji Park: Stroll through Tennoji Park, home to the Tennoji Zoo and beautiful cherry blossoms in spring.

Day 4:

Kyoto: Take a day trip to Kyoto, known for its rich cultural heritage.

Kinkaku-ji (Golden Pavilion): Visit the iconic Golden Pavilion, a Zen Buddhist temple covered in gold leaf.

Arashiyama Bamboo Grove: Explore the enchanting Arashiyama Bamboo Grove and visit the nearby Tenryu-ji Temple.

Gion District: Spend your evening in the Gion district, known for its traditional wooden machiya houses and geisha culture.

Judith G Harrison

DAY 5: NARA DAY TRIP

Nara: Another day trip, this time to Nara.

Nara Park: Discover Nara Park, home to hundreds of free-roaming deer and iconic landmarks like Todai-ji Temple.

Kasuga Taisha Shrine: Explore the beautiful Kasuga Taisha Shrine with its lantern-lined pathways.

Return to Osaka: Return to Osaka for a relaxing evening.

DAY 6: ART AND PARKS

Kuromon Ichiba Market: Begin your day with a visit to Kuromon Ichiba Market, where you can savor local street food.

Judith G Harrison

Osaka City Museum of Fine Arts: Delve into the Osaka City Museum of Fine Arts, showcasing a wide range of Japanese art.

Nagai Park: Spend your afternoon at Nagai Park, known for its botanical garden and the Nagai Botanical Garden Art Museum.

Dinner in Tenma: Enjoy dinner at one of the restaurants in the Tenma district, known for its vibrant nightlife.

DAY 7: MODERN AND CONTEMPORARY ART

Osaka Museum of History: Begin your day at the Osaka Museum of History, offering panoramic views of the city and insights into its past.

Hep Five Ferris Wheel: Take a ride on the Hep Five Ferris Wheel, offering stunning city views.

Minatomachi River Place: Explore the Minatomachi River Place and its galleries featuring contemporary art.

Farewell Dinner: Conclude your art-filled trip with a farewell dinner at a local restaurant.

3 AND 7 DAYS ITINERARY FOR FOODIES

3-day itinerary for foodies in Osaka, Japan.

DAY 1:

MORNING:

Judith G Harrison

- **Kuromon Ichiba Market:** Start your foodie adventure at Kuromon Ichiba Market, Osaka's culinary hub. Stroll through rows of stalls selling fresh seafood, street food, and local delicacies. Don't miss the chance to sample takoyaki (octopus balls), kushikatsu (deep-fried skewers), and fresh sashimi.

Lunch:

- **Sushi Hiro (Kuromon Ichiba Market):** Enjoy a lunch of delectable sushi and sashimi at Sushi Hiro. The market's fresh catches make this a sushi lover's paradise.

Judith G Harrison

AFTERNOON:

Dotonbori:

- After lunch, head to Dotonbori, Osaka's iconic entertainment district. Explore the vibrant streets filled with neon signs and street food vendors. Try the famous okonomiyaki (savory pancake) and takoyaki from local stalls.

EVENING:

- **Hozenji Yokocho:** Experience the cozy ambiance of Hozenji Yokocho, a historic alley filled with traditional izakayas and restaurants. Savor local dishes like yakitori (grilled skewers) and oden (hotpot).

DAY 2:

MORNING:

Judith G Harrison

- **Osaka Castle:** Start your day with a visit to Osaka Castle. While exploring the historical site, enjoy a traditional Japanese breakfast at a nearby restaurant.

Lunch:

- **Umeda Sky Building:** Head to the Umeda Sky Building for lunch at one of its top-floor restaurants. The panoramic views of Osaka complement the delicious cuisine.

AFTERNOON:

- **Daimaru Umeda:** Stroll around the Daimaru department store's food floors, where you can sample various regional Japanese dishes and pick up gourmet souvenirs.

Judith G Harrison

EVENING:

- **Kitashinchi District:** For dinner, venture to Kitashinchi, a district known for its upscale dining and intimate atmosphere. Try kaiseki (traditional multi-course meal) or opt for a teppanyaki experience.

Day 3: A Journey into Kyoto's Culinary Traditions

MORNING:

- **Day Trip to Kyoto:** Take a day trip to Kyoto, just a short train ride from Osaka. Begin your culinary exploration in this historic city.

Lunch:

- **Yudofu Sagano (Arashiyama):** Enjoy a traditional tofu-based meal, yudofu, at Yudofu Sagano in the scenic Arashiyama district.

AFTERNOON:

- **Kinkaku-ji (The Golden Pavilion):** Visit the iconic Kinkaku-ji, also known as the Golden Pavilion, and explore the temple's beautiful gardens.

EVENING:

- **GION DISTRICT:** Return to Osaka and spend your last evening in the Gion district, famous for geisha culture. Savor a Kyoto-style kaiseki dinner in one of the district's traditional restaurants.

7-day foodie itinerary for exploring the culinary delights of a city.

DAY 1: ARRIVAL AND LOCAL FLAVORS

- **Morning**: Arrive in the city and check-in to your accommodation.
- **Lunch**: Start your culinary journey with a local specialty. Ask locals for recommendations.
- **Afternoon**: Explore the local markets or food markets to get a taste of fresh produce and street food.
- **Dinner**: Try a traditional dinner at a local restaurant known for its regional cuisine.

DAY 2: BREAKFAST AND COOKING CLASS

- **Morning:** Begin your day with a hearty breakfast at a local cafe or bakery.

- **Late Morning:** Join a cooking class to learn how to prepare a local dish. This hands-on experience will give you insights into the local culinary culture.
- **Lunch**: Enjoy the fruits of your labor during the cooking class for lunch.
- **Afternoon**: Visit a food museum or culinary history center to delve into the city's food heritage.
- **Dinner**: Choose a restaurant known for fusion cuisine that blends local flavors with international twists.

DAY 3: STREET FOOD AND FOOD TOURS

- **Morning**: Start your day with a walking food tour, exploring local street food stalls and markets.
- **Lunch**: Sample a variety of street food items and regional specialties.

- **Afternoon**: Visit a food-themed museum or take a guided tour of a local food production facility (e.g., brewery, chocolate factory).
- **Dinner**: Dine at a highly-rated restaurant renowned for its innovative dishes.

DAY 4: ETHNIC CUISINE

- **Morning**: Enjoy breakfast at a cafe known for international cuisine.
- **Late Morning:** Explore the city's ethnic neighborhoods and choose a restaurant for a unique lunch experience (e.g., Thai, Italian, Ethiopian).
- **Afternoon**: Visit a spice market or specialty store to learn about exotic ingredients.
- **Dinner**: Try another ethnic restaurant or opt for a fusion restaurant that blends international flavors.

Judith G Harrison

DAY 5: FOOD MARKETS AND FOODIE SOUVENIRS

- **Morning**: Visit a local food market to pick up some fresh produce and culinary souvenirs.
- **Lunch**: Have a picnic at a nearby park with your market finds.
- **Afternoon**: Take a food photography class to capture the essence of your culinary journey.
- **Dinner**: Return to a favorite restaurant from earlier in the trip to savor another delightful meal.

DAY 6: FARM-TO-TABLE EXPERIENCE

- **Morning**: Participate in a farm-to-table experience, where you can harvest ingredients and prepare a meal with a local chef.
- **Lunch**: Enjoy the meal you prepared together with the chef.

- **Afternoon**: Explore nearby wineries, breweries, or olive groves for tastings and tours.
- **Dinner**: Choose a restaurant that emphasizes locally-sourced ingredients.

DAY 7: CULINARY WORKSHOPS AND FAREWELL DINNER

- Morning: Attend culinary workshops, such as pastry making or sushi rolling.
- Lunch: Savor the dishes you created during the workshops.
- Afternoon: Explore a local food market for some last-minute foodie souvenirs.
- Evening: End your foodie adventure with a farewell dinner at a Michelin-starred restaurant or a hidden gem that you discovered during your trip.

Judith G Harrison

CHAPTER 8: DAY TRIPS FROM OSAKA.

Osaka is not only a dynamic city in its own right but also an ideal gateway to the treasures of the Kansai region. In this chapter, we'll guide you through a selection of enriching day trips, allowing you to explore the cultural, historical, and natural wonders that lie just beyond Osaka's borders.

Kyoto: The Cultural Capital

A mere 30-minute train ride from Osaka brings you to Kyoto, the epitome of Japanese tradition and culture. Discover centuries-old temples, serene Zen gardens, and the allure of geisha culture in the historic Gion district. Whether you're admiring the vermilion gates of Fushimi Inari Shrine or sipping matcha in a traditional teahouse, Kyoto promises a profound immersion into Japan's rich heritage.

Nara: Ancient Temples and Deer Park

Judith G Harrison

Within an hour from Osaka, Nara welcomes you with open arms and adorable residents—free-roaming deer. Explore Nara Park, home to friendly deer that symbolize the city's spiritual connection. Visit Todai-ji Temple, housing the Great Buddha, and Kasuga Taisha Shrine, adorned with hanging lanterns. Nara's historic charm and natural beauty create an unforgettable day trip.

Kobe: City of Sake and Scenic Views

Judith G Harrison

Less than an hour from Osaka lies Kobe, a city known for its world-class beef and sake breweries. Savor a gourmet meal in Kobe's Chinatown, stroll along Harborland, and take in panoramic views from Mount Rokko. The Nunobiki Falls and Herb Gardens offer tranquil respites in the city's embrace.

Hiroshima and Miyajima Island:

A longer journey of about two hours leads to Hiroshima, a city with a poignant history and remarkable resilience. Pay your respects at the Hiroshima Peace Memorial Park and Museum,

Judith G Harrison

then take a ferry to Miyajima Island. Here, the iconic red torii gate seemingly floats on the water, and you can explore ancient shrines and hiking trails in a serene island setting.

Wakayama and Mount Koya:

Venture southward to Wakayama, where spiritual awakening awaits on Mount Koya (Koyasan). Accessible in under two hours, Koyasan is a sacred Buddhist pilgrimage site, replete with serene temple lodgings, lush cedar forests, and atmospheric cemeteries. Immerse yourself in the world of Japanese Buddhism through temple stays and contemplative walks.

These day trips from Osaka offer a rich tapestry of experiences, whether you seek cultural immersion, natural beauty, or historical insights. Each destination unveils a different facet of

Japan's cultural heritage, ensuring that your explorations beyond Osaka are as diverse and enriching as the city itself.

CHAPTER 9:

PRACTICAL INFORMATION

When exploring a new destination, having access to practical information can make your journey smoother and more enjoyable. In this chapter, we'll equip you with essential knowledge to navigate Osaka with confidence, covering everything from transportation to local customs.

Transportation in Osaka

Judith G Harrison

Osaka boasts a comprehensive public transportation system that includes subways, buses, and trains. Learn how to use the convenient prepaid IC cards like the "ICOCA" and "Osaka Amazing Pass" for hassle-free travel. Discover tips for navigating Osaka's well-connected subway system, and explore the option of renting bicycles to explore the city at your own pace.

Osaka Visitor Cards and Passes

Maximise your Osaka experience by utilizing visitor cards and passes. We'll guide you through the "Osaka Amazing Pass," which provides free access to various attractions and unlimited use of public transportation. Uncover other valuable city cards and discount passes to save both time and money during your stay.

Money and Currency Exchange

Osaka, like the rest of Japan, primarily uses cash for transactions. Discover where to find ATMs and currency exchange services. Understand the concept of Japanese yen and coins, and learn how to handle money respectfully in Japan, where cash is an essential part of daily life.

Safety and Emergency Contacts.

Judith G Harrison

Osaka is known for its safety, but it's important to be prepared. Familiarize yourself with emergency contacts, medical facilities, and common safety practices. Japan's low crime rate makes it a welcoming destination, but it's wise to be aware of local customs and emergency procedures.

Internet and Connectivity

Stay connected in Osaka by understanding your options for SIM cards, portable Wi-Fi devices, and free Wi-Fi hotspots. Whether you need internet access for navigation or communication, we'll provide guidance on staying connected throughout your trip.

Judith G Harrison

Local Etiquette and Customs

Respect for local customs and etiquette is essential when traveling in Japan. Learn about traditional greetings, bowing, and the art of gift-giving. Discover dining etiquette for eating in restaurants and izakayas, and understand the importance of removing your shoes when entering homes or certain establishments.

Judith G Harrison

Made in United States
Orlando, FL
11 March 2024

44574426R00104